Also by Marge Piercy

Fiction

GOING DOWN FAST
DANCE THE EAGLE TO SLEEP
SMALL CHANGES
WOMAN ON THE EDGE OF TIME
THE HIGH COST OF LIVING
VIDA
BRAIDED LIVES
FLY AWAY HOME

Poetry

BREAKING CAMP
HARD LOVING
TO BE OF USE
LIVING IN THE OPEN
THE TWELVE-SPOKED WHEEL FLASHING
THE MOON IS ALWAYS FEMALE
CIRCLES ON THE WATER
STONE, PAPER, KNIFE

Play

THE LAST WHITE CLASS (with Ira Wood)

Essays

PARTI-COLORED BLOCKS FOR A QUILT

My Mother's Body

MY MOTHER'S BODY

by Marge Piercy

ALFRED A. KNOPF   New York   1985

THIS IS A BORZOI BOOK
PUBLISHED BY ALFRED A. KNOPF, INC.

Library of Congress Cataloging in Publication Data
Piercy, Marge.   My mother's body.   I. Title.
PS3566.I4M9   1985   811'.54   84-48661
ISBN 0-394-54343-2
ISBN 0-394-72945-5 (pbk.)

Manufactured in the United States of America
Published April 9, 1985
Second Printing, August 1985

In Memory of my Mother

Bert Bernice Bunnin Piercy

and for my husband

Ira Wood

Contents

WHAT REMAINS

They inhabit me

I am pregnant with certain deaths
of women who choked before they
could speak their names
could know their names
before they had names to know.

I am owl, the spirit said,
I swim through the darkness on wide wings.
I see what is behind me
as well as what is before.
In the morning a splash of blood

on the snow marks where I found
what I needed. In the mild
light of day the crows mob
me, cursing. Are you the daughter
of my amber clock-tower eyes?

I am pregnant with certain deaths
of women whose hands were replaced
by paper flowers, which must be kept
clean, which could tear on a glance,
which could not hold even water.

I am cat. I rub your prejudices
against the comfortable way they grow.
I am fastidious, not as a careful
housewife, but as a careful lover,
keeping genitals as clean as face.

I turn up my belly of warm sensuality
to your fingers, purring my pleasure

and letting my claws just tip out.
Are you the daughter of the fierce
aria of my passion scrawled on the night?

I am pregnant with certain deaths
of women who dreamed that the lover
would strike like lightning and throw
them over the saddle and carry them off.
It was the ambulance that came.

I am wolf. I call across the miles
my messages of yearning and hunger,
and the snow speaks to me constantly
of food and want and friend and foe.
The iron air is heavy with ice

tweaking my nose and the sound
of the wind is sharp and whetted.
Commenting, chatting, calling,
we run through the net of scents
querying, Are you my daughter?

I am pregnant with deaths of certain
women who curled, wound in the skeins
of dream, who secreted silk
from spittle and bound themselves
in swaddling clothes of shrouds.

I am raccoon. I thrive in woods,
I thrive in the alleys of your cities.
With my little hands I open

whatever you shut away from me.
On your garbage I grow glossy.

Among packs of stray dogs I bare
my teeth, and the warring rats part.
I flourish like the ailanthus tree;
in your trashheaps I dig underground
castles. Are you my daughter?

I am pregnant with certain deaths
of women who wander slamming doors
and sighing as if to be overheard,
talking to themselves like water left
running, tears dried to table salt.

They hide in my hair like crabs,
they are banging on the nodes of my spine
as on the door of a tardy elevator.
They want to ride up to the observation
platform and peer out my eyes for the view.

All this wanting creates a black hole
where ghosts and totems whirl and join
passing through into antimatter of art,
the alternate universe in which such certain
deaths as theirs and mine throb with light.

The Annuity

1.

When I was fifteen we moved
from a tight asbestos shoebox
to a loose drafty two-story house,
my own tiny room prized under the eaves.
My privacy formed like a bud from the wood.

In my pale green womb I scribbled
evolving from worm to feral cat,
gobbling books, secreting bones,
building a spine one segment
at a time out of Marx and Freud.

Across the hall the roomers lived,
the couple from Appalachia who cooked
bacon in their room. At a picnic
she miscarried. I held her
in foaming blood. Lost twins.

Salesmen, drab, dirty in the bathroom,
solitary, with girly magazines,
detective stories and pads of orders,
invoices, reports that I would inherit
to write my poems on;

overgrown boys dogging you
out to the backyard with the laundry
baskets; middle-aged losers with eyes
that crawled under my clothes
like fleas and made me itch;

those who paid on time and those
with excuses breaking out like pimples
at the end of the month.
I slammed my door and left them,
ants on the dusty plain.

For the next twenty years
you toted laundry down two flights,
cleaned their bathroom every morning,
scrubbed at the butt burns,
sponged up the acid of their complaints

read their palms and gave common
sense advice, fielded their girlfriends,
commiserated with their ex-wives,
lied to their creditors, brewed
tisanes and told them to eat fruit.

What did you do with their checks?
Buy yourself dresses, candy, leisure?
You saved, waiting for the next depression.
You salted it away and Father took control,
investing and then spending as he chose.

2.

Months before you died, you had us drive
south to Florida because you insisted
you wanted to give me things I must carry back.
What were they? Some photographs, china

animals my brother had brought home from
World War II, a set of silverplate.

Then the last evening while Father watched
a game show, you began pulling out dollar
bills, saying *Shush, don't let him
see, don't let him know.* A five-dollar
bill stuffed under the bobbypins,
ten dollars furled in an umbrella,

wads of singles in the bottom of closet
dividers full of clothes. You shoved
them in my hands, into my purse,
you thrust them at Woody and me.
Take, you kept saying, *I want you to have
it, now while I can, take.*

That night in the hotel room
we sat on the floor counting money
as if we had robbed a candy store:
eighteen hundred in nothing larger
than a twenty, squirreled away, saved
I can't stand to imagine how.

That was the gift you had that felt
so immense to you we would need a car
to haul it back, maybe a trailer too,
the labor of your small deceit
that you might give me an inheritance,
that limp wad salvaged from your sweat.

Waking one afternoon
in my best dress

Until I tasted the blood spurt in my mouth
bursting its sour clots, and the air
forced my bucking lungs and I choked,
I did not know I had been dead.

The lint of voices consulting over me.
Didn't I leave myself to them,
an inheritance of sugared almond memories,
wedding cake slabs drying in their heads?
They carried me home and they ate me,
angel fluff with icing.

Now I return coiling and striking
on the slippery deck of dawn like a water
snake caught in a net, all fangs
and scales and slime and lashing tail.

I have crawled up from dankness
spitting headstones like broken teeth.
My breath spoils milk. My eyes
shine red as Antares in the scorpion's tail
and my touch sticks like mud.

I have been nothing
who now put on my body like an apron
facing a sink of greasy dishes.
Right here pain welded my ribs, here
my heart still smokes. My life hangs triggered
ready to trap me if I raise a hand.

Dresses flap and flutter about me
while my bones whistle

and my flesh rusts neuter as iron.
The rooms of my life wait
to pack me in boxes.

My eyes bleed. My eardrums
are pierced with a hot wire of singing
that only crows and hawks could harmonize.

My best dress splits from neck to hem.
Howling I trot for the brushlands with yellow
teeth blinking, hair growing out like ragweed
and new claws clicking on stone
that I must wear dull
before I can bear again
the smell of kitchens
the smell of love.

Out of the rubbish

Among my mother's things I found
a bottle-cap flower: the top
from a ginger ale
into which had been glued
crystalline beads from a necklace
surrounding a blue bauble.

It is not unattractive,
this star-shaped posy
in the wreath of fluted
aluminum, but it is not
as a thing of beauty
that I carried it off.

A receding vista opens
of workingclass making do:
the dress that becomes
a blouse that becomes
a doll dress, potholders,
rags to wash windows.

Petunias in the tire.
Remnants of old rugs
laid down over the holes
in rugs that had once
been new when the rem-
nants were first old.

A three-inch birch-bark
canoe labeled Muskegon,

little wooden shoes
souvenirs of Holland, Mich.,
an ashtray from the Blue Hole,
reputed bottomless.

Look out the window
at the sulphur sky.
The street is grey as
newspapers. Rats
waddle up the alley.
The air is brown.

If we make curtains
of the rose-bedecked table
cloth, the stain won't show
and it will be cheerful,
cheerful. Paint the wall lime.
Paint it turquoise, primrose.

How I used to dream
in Detroit of deep cobalt,
of ochre reds, of cadmium
yellow. I dreamed of sea
and burning sun, of red
islands and blue volcanos.

After she washed the floors
she used to put down newspapers
to keep them clean. When
the newspapers had become

dirty, the floor beneath
was no longer clean.

In the window, ceramic
bunnies sprouted cactus.
A burro offered fuchsia.
In the hat, a wandering Jew.
That was your grandfather.
He spoke nine languages.

Don't you ever want to
travel? *I did when I*
was younger. Now, what
would be the point?
Who would want to meet me?
I'd be ashamed.

One night alone she sat
at her kitchen table
gluing baubles in a cap.
When she had finished,
pleased, she hid it away
where no one could see.

Of pumpkins and ghosts I sing

Our Mardi Gras is this, not before
a season of fasting dictated once
by the bare cupboard of late winter,
but before the diet of thin gruel sun,
the winter putting it to us like a big
hard grey boot in the gut,
the storms that shovel us into their pit,
the snow that comes down like lace
and hardens to sludge in the gears:

A chance to be somebody else
before cabin fever turns you inside out
and counts your last resource
down to its copper head.
We dress like death whose time
of ascendance comes with the long
nights when the white moon freezes
on the snow and the fox hunts late,
his tail bannering, kill or starve.

I like the grinning pumpkinhead,
the skeleton mocking what will scatter it,
that puts on the face of its fears
and rollicks on the dead leaves
in the yard whooping and yowling.
Tonight you run in the streets,
brave because you wear a mask;

14

vampires do not worry about rape.
Witches wander the night like cats.

We bribe other people's children
with sweets not to attack us.
We put on sheets and cut eyeholes
although we all know that when ghosts
come, they wear their old clothes
and stand suddenly in the hall
looking for a boot or muse at the window
or speak abruptly out of their own
unused and unusable passion.

For my true dead I say kaddish
and light the yartzeit candle.
No, tonight it is our own mortality
we mock with cartoon grimace,
our own bones we peel to, dancing,
our own end we celebrate.
Long night of sugar and skull
when we put on death's clothes
and play act it like children.

Unbuttoning

The buttons lie jumbled in a tin
that once held good lapsang souchong
tea from China, smoky as the smell
from a wood stove in the country,
leaves opening to flavor and fate.

As I turn buttons over, they sound
like strange money being counted
toward a purchase as I point
dumbly in a foreign bazaar,
coins pittering from my hand.

Buttons are told with the fingers
like worry beads as I search
the trove for something small
and red to fill the missing
slot on a blouse placket.

I carried them from my mother's
sewing table, a wise legacy
not only practical but better
able than fading snapshots
to conjure buried seasons.

Button stamped with an anchor
means my late grade-school pea coat.
Button in the form of a white
daisy from a sky blue dress
she wore, splashed with that flower,

rouses her face like a rosy dahlia
bent over me petaled with curls.
O sunflower hungry for joy
who turned her face through the years
bleak, withered, still yearning.

The tea was a present I brought
her from New York where she
had never gone and never would.
This mauve nub's from a dress
once drenched in her blood;

This, from a coral dress she wore
the day she taught me that word,
summer '41, in Florida:
"Watch the clipper ships take off
for Europe. Soon war will come to us.

"They will not rise so peacefully
for years. Over there they're
killing us and nobody cares.
Remember always. Coral is built
of bodies of the dead piled up."

Buttons are useful little monuments.
They fasten and keep decently
shut and warm. They also open.
Rattling in my hand, they're shells
left by vanished flesh.

The sun and the moon
in the morning sky of Charlotte

for Julian Mason

The eye of fire and the eye of copper and blood
glared at each other through the veil of smog:
I woke from my too soft bed in the too warm motel
scheduled to rise between them as they tipped,

a balancing as of two balls at the farthest extremity
by a juggler momentarily lucky but about to lose one.
I rose under that influence balanced between blindness
and sight, between the hammered and nailed structure

of the self whose ark we labor at to save us
from drowning in the salty pit of memories
washed into that sea from distant and eroded
lives, and that rising tide and falling rain

in which hungers are circling up to feed.
I rose from a dream in which I came
over a burning plain and entered a wood
in which the corpses were tied up in trees

for the birds to clean. There I lay on a platform
awaiting the sharp beaks of the carrion eaters
for I understood my bones must be released
and the moon passed over me and drew up my blood

as mist and the sun passed over me and baked
the last sweet water from my tissues.
When the great crow landed on my face I cried
Not yet, not yet, and the crow asked, Will you not

give over? and I cried Not yet, not yet.
I woke on the red clay of Carolina trembling.
My life felt like a fragile silk chemise
I pulled on over my head to slip through the day.

As I stood among weeds and traffic I saw the red
moon and red sun eyeing each other, rivals
who should not be in the same room. I hoped
a moment ripens into death fulfilled

when I will say Yes, now; but death arrives
from within, without and sudden as a pasteboard
box crushed by a foot, and still I balance
in midlife praying, Not yet, not yet.

Putting the good things away

In the drawer were folded fine
batiste slips embroidered with scrolls
and posies, edged with handmade
lace too good for her to wear.

Daily she put on schmatehs
fit only to wash the car
or the windows, rags
that had never been pretty

even when new: somewhere
such dresses are sold only
to women without money to waste
on themselves, on pleasure,

to women who hate their bodies,
to women whose lives close on them.
Such dresses come bleached by tears,
packed in salt like herring.

Yet she put the good things away
for the good day that must surely
come, when promises would open
like tulips their satin cups

for her to drink the sweet
sacramental wine of fulfillment.
The story shone in her as through
tinted glass, how the mother

gave up and did without
and was in the end crowned

with what? scallions? crowned
queen of the dead place

in the heart where old dreams
whistle on bone flutes,
where run-over pets are forgotten,
where lost stockings go?

In the coffin she was beautiful
not because of the undertaker's
garish cosmetics but because
that face at eighty was still

her face at eighteen peering
over the drab long dress
of poverty, clutching a book.
Where did you read your dreams, Mother?

Because her expression softened
from the pucker of disappointment,
the grimace of swallowed rage,
she looked a white-haired girl.

The anger turned inward, the anger
turned inward, where
could it go except to make pain?
It flowed into me with her milk.

Her anger annealed me.
I was dipped into the cauldron
of boiling rage and rose
a warrior and a witch

but still vulnerable
there where she held me.
She could always wound me
for she knew the secret places.

She could always touch me
for she knew the pressure
points of pleasure and pain.
Our minds were woven together.

I gave her presents and she hid
them away, wrapped in plastic.
Too good, she said, too good.
I'm saving them. So after her death

I sort them, the ugly things
that were sufficient for every
day and the pretty things for which
no day of hers was ever good enough.

The Crunch

Like the cat the doberman has trapped,
like the rabbit in the fox's jaws
we feel the splintering of our bones
and wait for the moment that still may flash
the white space between pains
when we can break free.

It is the moment of damage
when already the pricing mind
tries to estimate cost and odds
while the nerves lean on their sirens
but the spine sounds a quiet tone
of command toward a tunnel of moment

that drills the air toward escape
or death. I have been caught.
Biology is destiny for all alive
but at the instant of tearing
open or free, the blood shrieks and
all my mother's mothers groan.

What remains

These ashes are not the fine dust I imagined.
The undertaker brings them out from the back
in a plastic baggie, like supermarket produce.
I try not to grab, but my need shocks me,
how I hunger to seize this officially
labeled garbage and carry you off.

All the water was vaporized,
the tears, the blood, the sweat,
fluids of a juicy, steamy woman
burnt offering into the humid Florida
air among cement palm trees with brown
fronds stuck up top like feather dusters.

In the wind the palmettoes clatter.
The air is yellowed with dust.
I carry you back North where you belong
through the bumpy black December night
on the almost empty plane stopping
at every airport like a dog at posts.

Now I hold what is left in my hands
bone bits, segments of the arched skull
varicolored stones of the body,
green, copper, beige, black, purple
fragments of shells eroded by storm
that slowly color the beach.

Archeology in a plastic baggie.
Grit spills into my palms:
reconstruct your days, your odyssey.
These are fragments of a smashed mosaic

that formed the face of a dancer
with bound feet, cursing in dreams.

At the marriage of the cat and dog
I howl under the floor.
You will chew on each other's bones
for years. You cannot read
the other's body language.
On the same diet you starve.

My longest, oldest love, I have brought
you home to the land I am dug into.
I promise a path laid right to you,
roses to spring from you, herbs nearby,
the company of my dead cats
whose language you already know.

We'll make your grave by piney woods,
a fine place to sit and sip wine,
to take the sun and watch the beans
grow, the tomatoes swell and redden.
You will smell rosemary, thyme,
and the small birds will come.

I promise to hold you in the mind
as a cupped hand protects a flame.
That is nothing to you. You cannot
hear. Yet just as I knew when you
really died, you know I have brought
you home. Now you want to be roses.

My mother's body

1.

The dark socket of the year
the pit, the cave where the sun lies down
and threatens never to rise,
when despair descends softly as the snow
covering all paths and choking roads:

then hawk-faced pain seized you
threw you so you fell with a sharp
cry, a knife tearing a bolt of silk.
My father heard the crash but paid
no mind, napping after lunch,

yet fifteen hundred miles north
I heard and dropped a dish.
Your pain sunk talons in my skull
and crouched there cawing, heavy
as a great vessel filled with water,

oil or blood, till suddenly next day
the weight lifted and I knew your mind
had guttered out like the Chanukah
candles that burn so fast, weeping
veils of wax down the chanukiyot.

Those candles were laid out,
friends invited, ingredients bought
for latkes and apple pancakes,
that holiday for liberation
and the winter solstice

when tops turn like little planets.
Shall you have all or nothing

take half or pass by untouched?
Nothing you got, *Nun* said the dreidl
as the room stopped spinning.

The angel folded you up like laundry
your body thin as an empty dress.
Your clothes were curtains
hanging on the window of what had
been your flesh and now was glass.

Outside in Florida shopping plazas
loudspeakers blared Christmas carols
and palm trees were decked with blinking
lights. Except by the tourist
hotels, the beaches were empty.

Pelicans with pregnant pouches
flapped overhead like pterodactyls.
In my mind I felt you die.
First the pain lifted and then
you flickered and went out.

2.

I walk through the rooms of memory.
Sometimes everything is shrouded in dropcloths,
every chair ghostly and muted.

Other times memory lights up from within
bustling scenes acted just the other side
of a scrim through which surely I could reach

my fingers tearing at the flimsy curtain
of time which is and isn't and will be
the stuff of which we're made and unmade.

In sleep the other night I met you, seventeen,
your first nasty marriage just annulled,
thin from your abortion, clutching a book

against your cheek and trying to look
older, trying to look middle class,
trying for a job at Wanamaker's,

dressing for parties in cast-off
stage costumes of your sisters'. Your eyes
were hazy with dreams. You did not

notice me waving as you wandered
past and I saw your slip was showing.
You stood still while I fixed your clothes,

as if I were your mother. Remember me
combing your springy black hair, ringlets
that seemed metallic, glittering;

remember me dressing you, my seventy-year-
old mother who was my last doll baby,
giving you too late what your youth had wanted.

3.

What is this mask of skin we wear,
what is this dress of flesh,
this coat of few colors and little hair?

This voluptuous seething heap of desires
and fears, squeaking mice turned up
in a steaming haystack with their babies?

This coat has been handed down, an heirloom,
this coat of black hair and ample flesh,
this coat of pale slightly ruddy skin.

This set of hips and thighs, these buttocks,
they provided cushioning for my grandmother
Hannah, for my mother Bert and for me

and we all sat on them in turn, those major
muscles on which we walk and walk and walk
over the earth in search of peace and plenty.

My mother is my mirror and I am hers.
What do we see? Our face grown young again,
our breasts grown firm, legs lean and elegant.

Our arms quivering with fat, eyes
set in the bark of wrinkles, hands puffy,
our belly seamed with childbearing.

Give me your dress so I can try it on.
Oh it will not fit you, Mother, you are too fat.
I will not fit you, Mother.

I will not be the bride you can dress,
the obedient dutiful daughter you would chew,
a dog's leather bone to sharpen your teeth.

You strike me sometimes just to hear the sound.
Loneliness turns your fingers into hooks
barbed and drawing blood with their caress.

My twin, my sister, my lost love,
I carry you in me like an embryo
as once you carried me.

4.

What is it we turn from, what is it we fear?
Did I truly think you could put me back inside?
Did I think I would fall into you as into a molten
furnace and be recast, that I would become you?

What did you fear in me, the child who wore
your hair, the woman who let that black hair

grow long as a banner of darkness, when you
a proper flapper wore yours cropped?

You pushed and you pulled on my rubbery
flesh, you kneaded me like a ball of dough.
Rise, rise, and then you pounded me flat.
Secretly the bones formed in the bread.

I became willful, private as a cat.
You never knew what alleys I had wandered.
You called me bad and I posed like a gutter
queen in a dress sewn of knives.

All I feared was being stuck in a box
with a lid. A good woman appeared to me
indistinguishable from a dead one
except that she worked all the time.

Your payday never came. Your dreams ran
with bright colors like Mexican cottons
that bled onto the drab sheets of the day
and would not bleach with scrubbing.

My dear, what you said was one thing
but what you sang was another, sweetly

subversive and dark as blackberries,
and I became the daughter of your dream.

This body is your body, ashes now
and roses, but alive in my eyes, my breasts,
my throat, my thighs. You run in me
a tang of salt in the creek waters of my blood,

you sing in my mind like wine. What you
did not dare in your life you dare in mine.

THE CHUPPAH

Dedicated to Rabbi Debra Hachen,
who made a beautiful wedding with us,
for which many of the poems in this section were written.
Two poems by Ira Wood are included.

Witnessing a wedding

Slowly and slower you have learned
to let yourselves grow while weaving
through each other in strong cloth.

It is not strangeness in the mate
you must fear, and not the fear
that loosens us so we lean back

chilly with a sudden draft on flesh
recently joined and taste again
the other sharp as tin in the mouth,

but familiarity we must mistrust,
the word based on the family
that fogs the sight and plugs the nose.

Fills the ears with the wax of possession.
Toughens the daily dead skin
callused against penetration.

Never think you know finally, or say
My husband likes, My wife is,
without balancing in the coil of the inner ear

that no one is surely anything till dead.
Love without respect is cold as a boa
constrictor, its caresses as choking.

Celebrate your differences in bed.
Like species, couples die out or evolve.
Ah strange new beasties with strawberry hides,

velvet green antlers, undulant necks,
tentacles, wings and the senses of bees,
your own changing mosaic of face

and the face of the stranger you live with
and try to love, who enters your body
like water, like pain, like food.

Touch tones

We learn each other in braille,
what the tongue and teeth taste,
what the fingers trace, translate
into arias of knowledge and delight
of silk and stubble, of bark
and velvet and wet roses,
warbling colors that splash through
bronze, violet, dragonfly jade,
the red of raspberries, lacquer, odor
of resin, the voice that later
comes unbidden as a Mozart horn
concerto circling in the ears.

You are translated from label,
politic mask, accomplished patter,
to the hands round hefting,
to a weight, a thrust, a scent
sharp as walking in early
morning a path through a meadow
where a fox has been last night
and something in the genes saying
FOX to that rich ruddy smell.
The texture of lambswool, of broadcloth
can speak a name in runes. Absent,
your presence carols in the blood.

The place where everything changed

Great love is an abrupt switching
in a life bearing along at express speeds
expecting to reach the designated stations
at the minute listed in the timetable.

Great love can cause derailment,
coaches upended, people screaming,
luggage strewn over the mountainside,
blood and paper on the grass.

It's months before the repairs are done,
everyone discharged from the hospital,
all the lawsuits settled, damage
paid for, the scandal subsided.

Then we get on with the journey
in some new direction, hiking overland
with camels, mules, via helicopter
by barge through canals.

The maps are all redrawn and what
was north is east of south
and there be dragons in those mountains
and the sun shines warmer and hairier

and the moon has a cat's face.
There is more sunshine. More rain.
The seasons are marked and intense.
We seldom catch colds.

There is always you at my back
ready to fight when I must fight;
there is always you at my side
the words flashing light and shadow.

What was grey ripples scarlet and golden;
what was bland reeks of ginger and brandy;
what was empty roars like a packed stadium;
what slept gallops for miles.

Even our bones are reformed in the close
night when we hold each other's dreams.
Memories uncoil backward and are remade.
Now the first egg itself is freshly twinned.

We build daily houses brick by brick.
We put each other up at night like tents.
This story tells itself as it grows.
Each morning we give birth to one another.

What Makes It Good?

What makes it good
Is that we came to this
Having each tasted freely
Of the sweet plum flesh of others.

So your head will not turn?
It may turn.
But my feet won't follow.

What makes it good
Is that we came to this slowly
Not blind or in white fever
Tearing off our clothes running
But walking arm around shoulder
Friends.

So you will not fight?
We will fight
Fists balled, throats
Full to choking
But we have learned
How to stop
Before the blade hits the throat.

What makes it good
Is that we give each other
Freedom, for the laughter
Of others.

So you've never had to give up friends?
I have given up
My gang of boys.
They wanted me to trade
Her for them
But why trade
When you have what you want?

What makes it good
Is that neither dawdles thinking
My lover kept me back.

So you are not ambitious?
I am ambitious.
And what will you do about her?
Take her with me.
And if you go nowhere?
It is no fault of hers.

What makes it good
Is that we
Both
Want it bad,
To be good.

                    Ira Wood

Why marry at all?

Why mar what has grown up between the cracks
and flourished, like a weed
that discovers itself to bear rugged
spikes of magenta blossom in August,
ironweed sturdy and bold,
a perennial that endures winters to persist?

Why register with the State?
Why enlist in the legions of the respectable?
Why risk the whole apparatus of roles
and rules, of laws and liabilities?
Why license our bed at the foot
like our Datsun truck: will the mileage improve?

Why encumber our love with patriarchal
word stones, with the old armor
of husband and the corset stays
and the chains of wife? Marriage
meant buying a breeding womb
and sole claim to enforced sexual service.

Marriage has built boxes in which women
have burst their hearts sooner
than those walls; boxes of private
slow murder and the fading of the bloom
in the blood; boxes in which secret
bruises appear like toadstools in the morning.

But we cannot invent a language
of new grunts. We start where we find
ourselves, at this time and place

which is always the crossing of roads
that began beyond the earth's curve
but whose destination we can now alter.

This is a public saying to all our friends
that we want to stay together. We want
to share our lives. We mean to pledge
ourselves through times of broken stone
and seasons of rose and ripe plum;
we have found out, we know, we want to continue.

We Come Together

We come together
Pure and ample
Top-heavy woman
Stocky man
Midwestern half-breed
Long Island Jew.

Jew with eyes of jade
Jew with eyes of almonds
Jews with tempers
Like the blue serpent tongue
Of the lightning that cracks
The sky over our land.

We come together strong
Strong as our passion to lie
Skin pressed to skin, quivering.
Strong as our hunger
To tell, to taste, to know.

I am lucky to have you
I know it.
But with each windfall
Comes the tax
With each rainfall
The weeds
To kneel and pull.

We give and take
With no line between.
We grow our food.
We heal our wounds.
You remind me

Good writing takes time,
I bolster you
When the world attacks.

We came together
Each an other,
Sister brother
Mother son
Father daughter
Man and woman.
We lick each other's skins like lost kittens.
Fight like starving strays.
We talk deep into the night
Make each other coffee
Keep each other straight.

We are scrub oak
Strong and low
Peony
Full bodied, brilliant
Feast for the butterfly
Feast for the ant.

Our love is like the land.
We work to keep it fertile.

Ira Wood

Every leaf is a mouth

The way the grain of you runs
wavy and strong as maple.

Black grapes warm in the hand,
the bloom on them like mist,

breathe their scent in gusts:
dusk of a summer evening.

In sleep you shimmer heat
banked like a Russian stove.

How wide you open to me,
a volcano gaping its belly

of fire all the way to the molten
core; a tree whose every leaf

is a mouth drinking sunshine
whose roots are all mouths.

Our life is a daily fugue
polyphonic, with odd harmonies

that make the bones vibrate
secretly, sweetly in the flesh

the way a divining rod shivers
over veins of water, or power.

The Wine

Red is the body's own deep song,
the color of lips, of our busy
organs, heart and stomach and lungs,
the color of our roused genitals,
the color of tongues and the flag of our blood.

Red is the loudest color
and the most secret
lurking inside the clothes' cocoon,
banked in the dark of the nightly bed
like coals shimmering in a stove.

It is the hot color, the active
that dances into your eye leaping,
that goads and pricks you
with its thorn of fire,
that shouts and urges and commands.

But red coils in the wineglass
head into tail like a dozing cat
whose eyes have shut but who purrs still
the pleasure of your hand, whose
warmth gently loosens the wine's aroma

so it rises like a perfumed ghost
inside the chambers of your nose.
In the mouth wine opens
its hundred petals like a damask rose
and then subsides, swallowed to afterglow.

In the wine press of the bed
of all the salty flows of our bodies,

the heat of our love ferments
our roundness into the midnight red
flowering of the wine

that can make drunken and make warm
that can comfort and quicken the sluggish
that can ease the weary body into sleep
that can frame the dark bread and cheese
into feast, that can celebrate

and sing through the wine of the body,
its own bright blood that rushes
to every cranny and cove of the flesh
and dark of the bone, the joy in love
that is the wine of life.

The Chuppah

The chuppah stands on four poles.
The home has its four corners.
The chuppah stands on four poles.
The marriage stands on four legs.
Four points loose the winds
that blow on the walls of the house,
the south wind that brings the warm rain,
the east wind that brings the cold rain,
the north wind that brings the cold sun
and the snow, the long west wind
bringing the weather off the far plains.

Here we live open to the seasons.
Here the winds caress and cuff us
contrary and fierce as bears.
Here the winds are caught and snarling
in the pines, a cat in a net clawing
breaking twigs to fight loose.
Here the winds brush your face
soft in the morning as feathers
that float down from a dove's breast.

Here the moon sails up out of the ocean
dripping like a just washed apple.
Here the sun wakes us like a baby.
Therefore the chuppah has no sides.

It is not a box.
It is not a coffin.
It is not a dead end.
Therefore the chuppah has no walls

We have made a home together
open to the weather of our time.
We are mills that turn in the winds of struggle
converting fierce energy into bread.

The canopy is the cloth of our table
where we share fruit and vegetables
of our labor, where our care for the earth
comes back and we take its body in ours.

The canopy is the cover of our bed
where our bodies open their portals wide,
where we eat and drink the blood
of our love, where the skin shines red
as a swallowed sunrise and we burn
in one furnace of joy molten as steel
and the dream is flesh and flower.

O my love O my love we dance
under the chuppah standing over us
like an animal on its four legs,
like a table on which we set our love
as a feast, like a tent
under which we work
not safe but no longer solitary
in the searing heat of our time.

How we make nice

Before we clean, we scream
accusatory, rowdy as gulls.
We screech, we bark, we flap.

Abruptly we subside and start.
Always it is two weeks past
the last endurable point.

It is destiny we grovel to,
that if we do not clean
we will smother in our own dirt.

We mutter and swot and heave.
We scrub and spray and haul out.
The vacuum cleaner chokes on a tissue

ball, its bag exploding; some cat
vomited behind the heaviest couch.
Dusted cobwebs fall on the scrubbed counter.

O house, neat as a stamp collection,
everything in its place ordained
glimmering with propriety at last.

Invite all our friends to dinner,
summon the neighbors who call
this the jungle. Let in the cats

to roll on the clean carpets.
By the next day it looks like
a rummage sale at five o'clock.

House-keeping

This box of house, like a child's
treasure trove of colored stones, blue jay
and pheasant feathers, random playing cards,
is irrational in the pleasure it proffers
those who fill it slowly
with the detritus and the clothing
of their living. It is the burrow
of a sand worm decorated with pebble
and shell the tides bring in.

This house is part toy: we move lamps
and chairs about exactly as I did
in my dollhouse, where I first played
at creation and fashioned dramas,
gave names to china animals, like Adam;
and like a god, invented rules.

This house is part clothing, a warm
coat that keeps us snug from the cold,
a huge raincoat that covers us dry.
It is our facade to friend and stranger,
stuck over with emblems of our taste,
our friends, our flush times, our travels,
our previous misadventures.

This house displays our virtue to each other.
I swept the kitchen floor twice this week.
But *I* took the trash to the dump Tuesday.
I am putting up shelves, so kiss me.
See how the freshly polished table shines
like a red, red apple with love.

This house is a nest in which the eggs
of worries hatch fledglings
of cowbird's young who usurp the care
and push the right nestlings out.
This house eats money and shits bills.

Bed, table, desk: here is the hearth of love.
I am territorial as my cats. When I return
I stroll the house singing arias of the familiar.
I leave here on a long tether that pulls
hard in the day and harder at night.

Return of the prodigal darling

At two a rabbit screamed.
A splash of blood on the floodlit needles.
The mice of the ashy dawn
nibbled my salted eyelashes.

Outside, the rough gears of the world
clanked on, bodies smashed
on every spoke and sprocket
oiling those grim wheels.

I dreamed your step, your warmth
against my side and woke to see
the weird grey stars of terror
wheeling around the pole of midnight.

The tears I spouted sleepless nights,
they are spangled on the grasses
among the small webs like flimsy tents,
now traps and prisms of the sun.

I am entire, grafted together,
satiated with you and shining
inside and outside, a hot orange,
liquid all through with joy.

Let me web and petal you with kisses,
let me deck you with love baubles
like a rich Christmas tree, hung
with totems and birds and lights.

My love is peeled to its prickly
bleeding quick. I want to lick you over
like a mother cat. Each hair of your
head is numbered in my love.

Down

Come let us raise our tent of skin.
Let me wrap you in the night of my hair
so our legs climb each other like pea vines.

The tiger lily is open on the freckled hour.
Bite into its ruddiness, a peach
splitting with ripeness and juice.

I stood in the sugar cane
near Cienfuegos and bit on the green
fibrous stem and the sweetness flowed.

We plunge into each other as into a pool
that closes over our heads. We float
suspended in liquid velvet.

The light comes from behind the eyes,
red, soft, thick as blood, ancient as sleep.
We build each other with our hands.

That is where flesh is translucent as water.
That is where flesh shines with its own light.
That is where flesh ripples as you walk

through it like fog and it closes around you.
That is where boundaries fail and wink out.
Flesh dreams down to rock and up to fire.

Here ego dissolves, a slug in vinegar,
although its loud demands will come back
like a bounced check as soon as we rise.

But this dim red place that waits at the pit
of the pool is real as the bone in the flesh
and there we make love as you make a table

where the blood roars like an ocean in the ears
remembering its source, and we remember
how we are bound and body of each other.

House built of breath

Words plain as pancakes syruped with endearment.
Simple as potatoes, homely as cottage cheese.

Wet as onions, dry as salt.
Slow as honey, fast as seltzer,

my raisin, my sultana, my apricot love
my artichoke, furry one, my pineapple

I love you daily as milk,
I love you nightly as aromatic port.

The words trail a bitter slime like slugs,
then in the belly warm like cabbage borscht.

The words are hung out on the line,
sheets for the wind to bleach.

The words are simmering slowly
on the back burner like a good stew.

Words are the kindling in the wood stove.
Even the quilt at night is stuffed with word down.

When we are alone the walls sing
and even the cats talk but only in Yiddish.

When we are alone we make love in deeds.
And then in words. And then in food.

The infidelity of sleep

We tie our bodies in a lover's
knot and then gradually uncoil.
We turn and talk, the night lapping
at the sills of the casements, rising
in us like dark heavy wine.

Then we turn aside. Eskimo
crawling into private igloos,
bears retreating to distant lairs,
a leopard climbing its home tree,
we go unmated into sleep.

In sleep you fret about who a lover
untouched for years is sleeping with.
Some man with a face glimpsed once
in a crowd lies over me sweating.
Now I wear male flesh like a suit of armor.

In sleep I am speaking French again.
The Algerian War is still on.
I curse, back to the wall of the top
floor of a workers'-quarter house.
The war in Vietnam is still on.

I am carrying a memorized message
to a deserter who is hiding
in a church belfry. All night
I drive fast down back roads
with a borrowed car full of contraband.

In the morning, of what we remember,
what can we tell? In the mind

dreams flash their facets, but in words
they dim, brilliant rocks picked up
at low tide that dry to mud.

Nightly the tides of sleep enter
us in secret claret-red oceans
from whose deep slide serpents
wearing faces radiant and impure
as saints in Renaissance paintings.

Now as night pours in to fill the house
like a conch shell, we cling together,
muttered words between us, a spar
we hold to knowing that soon
we will let go, severed, to drown.

Nailing up the mezuzah

A friend from Greece
brought a tin house
on a plaque, designed
to protect our abode,
as in Greek churches
embossed legs or hearts
on display entreat aid.
I hung it but now
nail my own proper charm.

I refuse no offers of help,
at least from friends,
yet this presence
is long overdue. Mostly
we nurture our own
blessings or spoil them,
build firmly or undermine
our walls. Who are termites
but our obsessions gnawing?

Still the winds blow hard
from the cave of the sea
carrying off what they will.
Our smaller luck abides
like a worm snug in an apple
who does not comprehend
the shivering of the leaves
as the ax bites hard
in the smooth trunk.

We need all help proffered
by benign forces. Outside

we commit our beans to the earth,
the tomato plants started
in February to the care
of the rain. My little
pregnant grey cat offers
the taut bow of her belly
to the sun's hot tongue.

Saturday I watched alewives
swarm in their thousands
waiting in queues quivering
pointed against the white
rush of the torrents
to try their leaps upstream.
The gulls bald as coffin
nails stabbed them casually
conversing in shrieks, picnicking.

On its earth, this house
is oriented. We grow
from our bed rooted firmly
as an old willow into the water
of our dreams flowing deep
in the hillside. This hill
is my temple, my soul.
Malach hamoves, angel of death
pass over, pass on.

CHIAROSCURO

The good go down

I build stories. They own
their own shapes, their rightful
power and impetus, plot
them however I try, but always
that shape is broadly just.

I want to believe in justice
inexorable as the decay
of an isotope; I want to plot
the orbit of justice, erratic
but inevitable as a comet's return.

It is not blind chance I rail at,
the flood waters that carry off
one house and leave its neighbor
standing one foot above the high
water's swirling grasp.

It is that the good go down
not easily, not gently,
not occasionally, not by random
deviation and the topple
of mischance, but almost always.

Here is something new and true.
No, you are too different,
too raw, too spiced and gritty.
We want one like the last one.
We know how to sell that.

We want one that praises us,
we want one that puts down

the ones we squat on, no
aftertaste, no residue of fine
thought smeared on the eyes.

We want one just like all
the others, but with a designer
label and a clever logo.
We want one we saw advertised
in *The New York Times*.

Are the controls working?
Is the doorman on duty?
Is the intercom connected?
Is the monitor functioning?
Is the incinerator on?

It goes without saying:
The brie shall be perfectly
ripe, the wine shall be a second
cru Bordeaux from a decent year,
there shall be one guest

with a recent certified success
and we shall pass around plates
of grated contempt for those
who lack this much, of sugared
envy for those who have more.

For the young not facile enough
to imitate the powerful, not skilled

enough liars to pretend sucking them
is ecstasy, they erect a massive
wall, the Himalayas of exclusion.

For the old who speak too much
of pain, they have a special
Greenland of exile. Old Birnbaum.
Nobody reads her anymore.
I thought she was dead.

Once she is, and her cat
starves, she will become a growth
industry. Only kill yourself
and you can be consumed too,
an incense-proffered icon.

It is the slow mean defeat
of the good that I rail against,
the small pallid contempt of the well
placed for those who do not lack
the imaginative power to try,

the good who are warped by passion
as granite is twisted into mountains
and metamorphosed by fire into marble;
who speak too loud in vulgar tongues
because they have something to say;

who mean what they make down to their
bones; who commit the uncouth error

of feeling, of saying what they feel,
of making others feel. Their reward
is to be made to feel worthless.

Goodness is not dangerous enough.
I want goodness like a Nike armed
with the warhead of rightful anger.
I want goodness that can live on sand
and stones and wring wine from burrs,

goodness that can put forth fruit,
manured with the sewage of hatred.
The good must cultivate their anger
like fields of wheat that must feed
them, if they are ever to win.

Homage to Lucille,
Dr. Lord-Heinstein

We all wanted to go to you.
Even women who had not heard
of you, longed for you, our
cool grey mother who would
gently, carefully and slowly, using
no nurse but ministering herself,
open our thighs and our vaginas
and show us the os smiling
in the mirror like a full rising moon.

You taught us our health, our sickness
and our regimes, presiding over
the raw ends of life, a priestess eager
to initiate. Never did you tell us
we could not understand what you
understood. You made our bodies
glow transparent. You did not think
you had a license to question us
about our married state or lovers' sex.

Your language was as gentle and caring
as your hands. On the mantel
in the waiting room the clippings hung,
old battles, victories, marches.
You with your flower face, strong
in your thirties in the thirties,
were carted to prison for the crime

of prescribing birth control
for workingclass women in Lynn.

The quality of light in those quiet
rooms where we took our shoes off
before entering and the little
dog accompanied you like a familiar,
was respect: respect for life,
respect for women, respect for choice,
a mutual respect I cannot imagine
I shall feel for any other doctor,
bordering on love.

Where is my half-used tube
of Tom's fennel toothpaste tonight?

Here I am I think in Des Moines,
in Dubuque, in Moscow Idaho, in a cube of motel room
but where is my wandering luggage tonight?

Where is my bathrobe slippery as wet rock,
green as St. Patrick's Day icing?
Are my black boots keeled over under another bed?
Do my tampons streak across the night
little white rockets trailing contrails of string?
Are women in Alaska dicing for my red shoes?
Did TWA banish my suitcase to Siberia?

Where is that purple dress in which my voice
is twice as loud, with the gold belt
glittering like the money I hope to get paid,
sympathetic magic to lure checks
out of comptrollers before time molders?

I feel like an impostor, a female impersonator,
a talking laundry bag dialing head calls
to all my clothes in Port Huron, in Biloxi, in Tucson,
collect calls into the night: I'm lonely and dirty.
I'm sorry I spilled chili on you, chocolate sauce,
Elmer's Glue. I'll wear an apron at all times.
I'll never again eat tacos. O my wandering clothes,
fly through the night to me, homing pigeons
trailing draperies like baroque saints, come home.

Your cats are your children

Certain friends come in, they say
Your cats are your children.
They smile from a great height on down.
Clouds roll in around their hair.
I have real children, they mean,
while you have imitation.

My cats are not my children.
I gave Morgaine away yesterday
to a little boy she liked.
I'm not saving to send them to Harvard.
When they stay out overnight
I don't call the police.

I like the way they don't talk,
the way they do, eyes shining
or narrowed, tails bannering,
paws kneading, cats with private
lives and passions sharp as their claws,
hunters, lovers, great sulkers.

No, my children are my friends,
my lover, my dependents on whom
I depend, those few for whom
I will rise in the night to give
comfort, massage, medicine,
whose calls I always take.

My children are my books
that I gestate for years,
a slow-witted elephant
eternally pregnant, books

that I sit on for eras like the great
auk on a vast marble egg.

I raise them with loving care,
I groom and educate them,
I chastise, reward and adore.
I exercise them lean and fatten them up.
I roll them about my mind all night
and fuss over them in the mornings.

Then they march off into the world
to be misunderstood, mistreated, stolen,
to be loved for the wrong reasons,
to be fondled, beaten, lost.
Now and then I get a postcard
from Topeka Kansas, doing just fine.

People take them in and devour them.
People marry them for love.
People write me letters and tell me
how they are my children too.
I have children whose languages
rattle dumbly in my ears like gravel,

children born of the wind that blows
through me from the graves of the poor
and brave who struggled all their short
throttled lives to free people
whose faces they could not imagine.
Such are the children of my words.

Mr. Big

Darkest chocolate, bittersweet,
the muscled power of horse's
haunches, the sleekness of a seal,
the swagger of a heavyweight
strolling to the ring:

Jim Beam works hard as overlord
hustling to rule his turf in winter
when only the great horned owl
can frighten him. But July Fourth
brings up the summer people

with their dogs, their cats,
their children, their dirt bikes,
their firecrackers. All summer
he collects scars and anger
trying to boss his ward.

He gets leaner, meaner.
He sulks and roars in baritone
O my unappreciated soul, all night.
He wants to be force-fed
love like chicken soup.

He wants love to chase him
like a panting dog,
without asking, without earning.
Jim Beam, you're indistinguishable
from half the men I've adored.

Being a cat you are lucky.
I do carry you off by force
and today you lie by the computer
on a satin pillow and eat turkey
and suffer, suffer your belly

to be scratched and endure
your chin chucked and tickled, at ease,
air conditioned while it's ninety out.
O Jim Beam, this must
be love: will you marry me?

The maternal instinct at work

In the bed Dinah curls,
kittens tumbling over kittens
at nipples pink and upright
against the silver blue fur.
Her mrow interrogates.

The second night she toted
them one by one into my bed
arranged them against my flank
nuzzling, then took off
flirting her tail.

Birthing box, bottoms
of closets, dark places,
the hell with that. She
crawled between my legs
when her water broke.

Think of them as *ours*
she urges us, have you
heard of any decent day care?
I think kitten raising
should be a truly collective

process, and besides, it's all
your fault. You gave me
to that little silver-
balled brute to do his will
upon me. Now look.

Here I am a hot-water
bottle, an assembly line
of tits, a milk factory.
The least you can do
is take the night feeding.

Magic mama

The woman who shines with a dull comfortable glow.
The woman who sweats honey, an aphid
enrolled to sweeten the lives of others.

The woman who puts down her work like knitting
the moment you speak, but somehow it gets done
secretly in the night while everyone sleeps.

The woman whose lap is wide as the Nile
delta, whose flesh is a lullaby
of goosedown petals lacking the bite

of menace real lullabies ride on
(if the bough breaks, birds
and butterflies pecking out his eyes).

Whose own eyes are soft-focus mirrors.
Whose arms are bolsters. Whose love
is laid on like the municipal water.

She is not the mother goddess, vortex
of dark and light powers with her consorts,
her hungers, her favorites, her temper

blasting the corn so it withers in its ear,
her bloody humor that sends the hunter fleeing
to be tracked and torn by his hounds,

the great door into the earth's darkness
where bones are rewoven into wheat,
who loves the hawk as she loves the rabbit.

Big mama has no power, not even over herself.
The taxpayer of guilt, whatever she gives
you both agree is never enough.

She is a one-way street down which pour
parades of opulent gifts and admiration
from a three-shift factory of love.

Magic mama has to make it right, straighten
the crooked, ease pain, raise the darkness,
feed the hungry and matchmake for the lonesome

and ask nothing in return. If you win
you no longer know her, and if you lose
it is because her goodness failed you.

Whenever you create big mama from another
woman's smile, a generosity of spirit working
like yeast in the inert matter of the day,

you are stealing from a woman her own ripe
grape sweet desire, the must of her fears,
the shadow she casts into her own future

and turning her into a diaper service,
the cleaning lady of your adventure.
Who thanks a light bulb for giving light?

Listen, your mother is not your mother.
She is herself and unmothered. It is time
to take the apron off your mind.

Nothing more will happen

You are rumpled like a sweater
smelling of burnt leaves and dried sea grasses.
Your smile belongs to an archaic boy of wasting stone
     on Delos.
You change shape like spilled mercury.
There is no part of you that touches me
not even your laugh catching like fur in your nose.

I am with you on a glacier
white snowfield gouged with blue-green crevasses
deep and the color of your eyes.
There is no place to go, we cannot lie down.
In the distance your people wait checking their gear.
We blaze like a refinery on the ice.

A dry snow begins to descend
as your hands fall clasped to your sides
as your eyes freeze to the rim of the sky.
Already I cannot see you for the snow.
Heavy iron gates like those in a levee or fortress
are closing in my breasts.

Blue Tuesday in August

The world smelled like a mattress you find
on the street and leave there,
or like a humid house reciting yesterday's
dinner menu and the day before's.
Everybody had breathed this air repeatedly
and used it to cool an engine.
Oil hung in the sky in queasy clouds.
Then the rain swept through slamming doors.

Today is blue as a cornflower,
tall as a steel tower,
springy as a trampoline.
Beside the drive the ruffs of Queen Anne's lace
are host to the striped caterpillar
that probes with its roan horns.
Dry as the white dunes under sunlight, the day
smells of cut curing grasses beige as Siamese cats.

The cicadas like little chainsaws inflame the air.
All things bear sharp corners of a pane of glass.
What a clean unused day to walk all over.
On such a morning I can almost believe
something blue and green and yellow
may survive us after we explode
and burn the sky down.
Some shoot may sprout and grow.

The Disinherited

We do not inherit the world from our parents,
we borrow it from our children.

Gandhi

The dreams of the children
reek of char and ashes.

The fears of the children
peer out through the brown eyes

of a calf tethered away from its mother,
a calf who bawls for the unknown

bad thing about to happen
as the butcher's truck arrives.

The children finger their own sharp
bones in their wrists.

They knead their foreheads gingerly.
Last night I dreamed Mother was burning,

the little girl said in class,
my father, my dog, my brother,

fire was eating them all.
I wrote three postcards to the President.

I won't be anything when I grow up,
the boy said, I won't live that long.

I don't like firecrackers anymore.
I always draw houses falling.

Blood seeps from the roof of the cave
of their minds, fear becoming rock.

In their dreams there is one great
loud noise. Then weeping. Then silence.

Cold head, cold heart

I suppose no one has ever died of a head cold
while not fearing or fervently
wishing to do so on the hour,
gasping through a nose the size of Detroit.

My mouth tastes of moldy sneaker.
My tongue is big as a liverwurst.
My throat steams like a sewer.
The gnome of snot has stuck a bicycle pump in my ear.

I am a quagmire, a slithy bog.
I exude effluvia, mumbled curses,
and a dropsy of wads of paper,
handkerchiefs like little leprosies.

The world is an irritant
full of friends jumping in noisy frolic.
The damned healthy: I breathe on them.
My germs are my only comfort.

Deferral

You'll do it, what you really want.
You'll start counting, you'll
feel everything direct as rain
on your skin in mild May twilight.
You'll start chewing every moment
like fresh corn on the cob hot
buttered and actually enjoy it
as soon as you grow up, leave home,
after you've got your diploma,
when you've passed your orals,
when you finish psychoanalysis,
as soon as you meet the one woman for you,
when Mr. Right comes charging along,
after you pay off the mortgage,
as soon as the children are in school,
when you finally get the divorce,
after the children finish college,
when you're promoted as you deserve,
when you're a complete success at last,
after you retire to Florida,
when you die and go to heaven.
You'll have considerable practice
at being dead by then.

Breaking out

My first political act? I am seeing
two doors that usually stood open,
leaning together like gossips, making
a closet of their corner.

A mangle stood there, for ironing
what I never thought needed it:
sheets, towels, my father's underwear;

an upright vacuum with its stuffed
sausage bag that deflated with a gusty
sigh as if weary of housework as I,
who swore I would never dust or sweep

after I left home, who hated
to see my mother removing daily
the sludge the air lay down like a snail's track

so that when in school I read of Sisyphus
and his rock, it was her I
thought of, housewife scrubbing
on raw knees as the factories rained ash.

Nasty stork king of the hobnobbing
doors was a wooden yardstick dusty
with chalk marks from hems' rise and fall.

When I had been judged truly wicked
that stick was the tool of punishment.
I was beaten as I bellowed like a locomotive
as if noise could ward off blows.

My mother wielded it more fiercely
but my father far longer and harder.
I'd twist my head in the mirror to inspect.

I'd study those red and blue mountain
ranges as on a map that offered escape,
the veins and arteries the roads
I could travel to freedom when I grew.

When I was eleven, after a beating
I took and smashed the ruler to kindling.
Fingering the splinters I could not believe.

How could this rod prove weaker than me?
It was not that I was never again beaten
but in destroying that stick that had measured my pain
the next day I was an adolescent, not a child.

This is not a tale of innocence lost but power
gained: I would not be Sisyphus.
There were things that I should learn to break.

Paper birds

Paper birds:
can they fly?
Not far.

Can they dive after fish?
Do they lay edible eggs?
Do they eat harmful insects?

No, but they sing
both long and short
and scratch real fleas.

Can you cook them?
How do they taste?
Like you. Like me.

They fill the mind
but half an hour later
you want more.

How many kinds are there?
They evolve, like other
birds, fill empty niches,

become extinct.
But each species
is composed of only one.

How do they reproduce then?
By fission. By fusion.
By one hell of a lot of work.

Listening to a speech

The woman carefully dressed
in quasimale drag
fashionable among her friends
spoke scornfully from the podium
of bourgeois housewives.

Bourgeois? Someone who works
for nothing
who owns zip,
who receives no pension,
who possesses no credit, no name.

I thought the bourgeoisie
owned the means of production?
She is a means of reproduction
leased by her husband,
liable to be traded in.

Those widows who live on cat food,
those ladies who eat in cafeterias
once a day, taking fifteen
minutes to choose their only dish,
their houses have deserted them.

This bag lady chewing stale hot-
dog buns from the garbage igloo,

who pees in the alley squatting,
who sleeps in an abandoned car,
was a bourgeois housewife.

Your superiority licks itself
like a pleased cat. No housewife
is bourgeois any more than pets
are, just one owner away
from the streets and starvation.

Making a will

Over the shoulder peer cartoon images
of skinny misers and bloated bankers
disinheriting wayward daughters in love
with honest workingclass boys;
the dowager in her bed writing in
the gardener, writing out her nephew.

Little goes the way we plan it
even with us to knead and pull,
stir and sweeten and cook it down.
How many scenes written flat on the back
in bed ever play in the moonlight?
How often revenge bubbles itself flat.

Given wobbly control with all our
muscle and guile and wit bearing down
like a squad of tactical police,
how do we suppose when we're ashes
what we think we want will matter?
Less than the spider in the rafters.

We cannot protect those we love
no matter how we gild and dip them
in the molten plastic of our care;
when we are gone our formulae
in legal sludge guarantee nothing
but that all lawyer's fees be paid.

Maybe it is an act of faith
not in anything but the goodwill
of a few, those documents of intent

we scatter in which we claim sound mind
and try to stuff a log in the jaws
of fate to keep those teeth from closing.

Our will dies with us indeed, although
consequences resonate through the stars
with old television dramas,
undergoing a red shift we will never
comprehend as distance bends our acts,
our words, our memories, to alien

configurations fading into lives
of creatures strange to us as jellyfish
in a future we have hewn, bled,
bounded and escaped from. What
we have truly bequeathed is what
we have done or neglected, to that end.

Still life

We have glass eyes and rubber fingers.
Our minds are industrial dumps,
full of chemical residues, reruns,
jeans commercials and the asses
of people we have never touched.
The camera sees for us.
Our pets act out our emotions.

Quiet has to be waited into.
Can I learn to coil, a snake
on a warm flat rock? Can I stand
eyes and ears open
hands up like a daisy?
Can I learn to see what the fox
contemplates, paws tucked and smiling?

My bones have forgotten
how to fall through the moment
to float leaf-light and land
like a sheet of paper.
Will a teacher come
if I wait in the orange light
on top of this dune?

See the sparrow hawk stand in the air
balancing the keel of her breastbone
on the surges of wind and warmth:
till she strikes hard,
how the pressures sustain her
exact and teetering
on blurred wings.

From HoJo's to Mr. Softee

When vittles must keep on a shelf for years
like newsprint slowly yellowing, when food
can't be bitter or spicy or hot or sour,
then people drink sweet pop, gobble sweet cupcakes
under icings and pour sugar on presweetened
breakfast crunchies and eat iceberg lettuce
with thick orange corn-syrup dressing, sugar
in the hamburgers and fish sticks.

Swelling in our soft mounded flesh, instead
of ornery people, we want our food to love us.
The child learns: Love is sugar.
She grows up sucking, chewing, nibbling
and is still and always hungry in her cancerous
cells busy and angry as swarming ants.

The longings of women

The longings of women:
butterflies beating against
ceilings painted blue like sky;
flies buzzing and thumping their heads
against the pane to get out.
They die and are swept off
in a feather duster.

The hopes of women are pinned
after cyanide by rows
labeled in Latin
the fragile wings fading.
The keeper speaks with melancholy
of how beautiful they were
as if he had not killed them.

The anger of women runs like small
brown ants you step on,
swarming in cracks in the pavement,
marching in long queues
through the foundation and inside,
nameless, for our names
are not yet our own.

But we are many and hungry
and our teeth though small are sharp.
If we move together
there is no wall we cannot erode
dust-grain by speck, and the lion
when he lies down is prey
to the army of ants.

Out of sight

Put away.
They do that to pets:
He was suffering. We
had him put away.
They do that to women: She wouldn't
do the dishes, she heard Saint
Catherine telling her to prophesy in the street.
He had her put away.

Refuse: the garbage, that
which is refused, which is denied,
which is discarded.

The crime of the women in the locked ward
was asking for help.
If you beg from the wrong people
they chop off your hands,
the old woman said to me.
My companion made a sign
with her fingers, but I did
not think the old lady
mistaken. Her hands rattled
like dead leaves from Thorazine.
She said, I can't hold a pen
but it can hold me.

The powerful make and break laws.
The weak flee to the bus

station, their purses stuffed
with tissues and old letters.

The weak rush into the closet
where the dresses smell like Mother,
into the mirror and through the wall
into the maze of dreams.

You are punished for wrong thinking
by having your brain burnt out
as the Koran bids you cut off
the hand of a thief.
The bodies of the witches were burned
alive in the millions. What
barbarity. We burn only brains.

Does the light fail us,
or do we fail the light?

1.

My old cat lives under a chair.
Her long fur conceals the sharp
jut of her fleshless bones.

Her eyes are dimmed by clouds
of cataract, only visible
if you remember their willow green

as I could judge my mother's
by calling up that fierce charred
brown gaze, smiting, searching.

When one of the young cats approaches
she growls in anger harmless
as distant thunder. They steal her food.

They do not act from malice.
They would curl up with her and wash.
She hisses fear. Her lifelong

companion died. They appeared.
Surely the young bear the blame
for all the changes that menace

in the fog of grey shapes looming.
Her senses that like new snow
had registered the brush strokes

of tracks, the fall of a pine needle,
the alighting of a chickadee;
her senses that had opened

greedy as the uncurling petals
of a sea anemone that drinks
the world's news from the current;

that tantalized her with message
of vole and shrew and rabbit,
boasting homage her lovers sprayed,

have failed her like an old
hanging bridge that decays
letting her drop through in terror

to the cold swift river beneath.
In her ears is her blood rushing.
The light is trickling away.

2.

One day this week my father
briefly emerged from the burrow
he bought himself lined with nurses.

When he gets me on the phone
he never believes it's me.
When I insist, he swells with anger.

He really wants to phone my mother.
Often he calls me by her name
but every time I fail him.

I am the dead woman in body,
hips and breasts and thighs,
elbows and chin and earlobes,

black black hair as at the age
she bore me, when he still
loved her, here she stands,

but when I open my mouth
it's the wrong year and the world
bristles with women who make short

hard statements like men and don't
apologize enough, who don't cry
when he yells or makes a fist.

He tells me I have stolen his stamps
down in Florida, the bad utopia
where he must share a television.

You took my nail scissors, he shouts
but means I stole his vigor
deposited in his checkbook like a giant's

external soul. I have his checkbook
and sign, power of attorney,
as I pay his doctors, doctors,

doctors, as I hunch with calculator
trying to balance accounts. We each
feel enslaved to the other's will.

3.

Father, I don't want your little pot
of nuggets secreted by bad living
hidden in the mattress of Merrill Lynch

in an account you haven't touched
for twenty years, stocks that soared,
plummeted, doddering along now

in their own mad dinosaur race.
That stock is the doctor that Mother
couldn't call when she had the first

stroke, the dress she didn't get,
at eighty-six still scrubbing, cooking,
toting heavy laundry. The dentist

I couldn't go to so I chewed
aspirin as my teeth broke
at fifteen when I went out to work,

all the pleasures, the easing of pain
you could have bought with both
your endless hard mutual labor.

The ghostly dust bowl roared in the mind
afterward, the desert of want
where you would surely perish and starve

if you did not hide away pennies of power,
make do, make do, hold hard,
build a fortress of petrified dollars

stuck together like papier-mâché
so the tempest of want
could be shut out to howl at others.

Dirty little shacks, a rooming-
house Mother ran for decades,
a trailer park; after she died

you bought into Total Life Care,
a tower of middle-class comfort
where you could sit down to lunch

declaring, My broker says.
But nobody would listen. Only
Mother had to listen and she is dead.

You hid alone in your room fighting
with the cleaning woman who came
each week but didn't do it right,

then finally one midnight wandered out naked
finally to the world among rustling
palms demanding someone make you lunch.

4.

I wouldn't sign papers to commit
you but they found a doctor who would.
Now you mutter around the ward,

This was supposed to be fun.
Do you see your future in the bent
ones who whimper into their laps,

who glare at walls through which
the faces of the absent peer, who hear
conspiracy mutter in the plumbing?

I am the bad daughter who could speak
with my mother's voice if I wanted,
because I wear her face, who ought

to be cooking your meals, who ought
to be running the vacuum you bought
her, but instead I pretend

I am married, pretend to be writing
books and giving speeches.
You won't forgive her ever for dying

but I heard you call the night nurse
by her name. You speak of the fog
you see in the room. Greyness

is blowing in, the fog that took
my mother while you slept,
the fog that shriveled your muscles,

the fog that thickens between you
and strangers here where all
is provided and nothing is wanted.

The sun blasts on, flat and blatant.
Everything was built yesterday
but you. Nobody here remembers

the strike when you walked the picket line
joking with sleet freezing your hair,
how you stood against the flaming wall

of steel and found the cracked bearing,
how you alone could make the old turbines
turn over, how you had the wife

other men watched when she swayed
over the grass at the company picnic,
how you could drink them all witless.

You're a shadow swallowed by fog.
Through your eyes it enters your brain.
When it lifts you see only pastel

walls and then your anger standing there
gleaming like a four-hundred-horsepower car
you have lost your license to drive.

UNDERRATED PLEASURES

Building is taming

Once a hillside above a marsh,
a swell of sand and clay sprouting
pines, white oaks, blueberry bushes.
A friend who came along to view
the lot pissed into the bushes.
A red-shouldered hawk rose
from a rabbit carcass furious
sputtering and wet.

Yet when the builders finished
the land was undone,
the house a box gouged into sand,
the hillside stripped
washing down into the road below.

I planted and terraced to hold
the land. Then this became
my only graphic artwork,
painting with greys and greens,
the four-dimensional sculpture
of the garden, every two weeks recoloring,
the angular, the globular,
the tousled, the spiky, the lush.
Collage of fragrances, sweet,
spicy, acrid, subtle, banging.

Once I watched my female Burmese
Colette pass along the herb
garden savoring, rubbing her cheek
into the funky leaves, but at the anise
hyssop she sniffed at it and hissed,

as if its odor spoke to her rudely.
Cats would have a thousand names for scent.

Dogwood, honeysuckle, autumn olive
bore berries and summoned birds
to stir the air of the hillside,
to scuttle in the underbrush kicking
up leaves, to flit through branches.

Every person who has lived here
has carved initials on the land:
that path, that fence, those steps, that shed.
What draws the eye and hand initially,
what charms, is after we move in
changed by us.

The lover alters
the beloved by her love,
even by that hot and tender regard.
What we make is part the other
and part us, and what we become
in our new love is someone
born from both.

Cowering in a corner

A spider nests in the frying pan
this Wednesday morning; a jumping
spider stalks prey on the window
ledge among bottles; little black
spider is suddenly swimming
in my wineglass; hairy king
kong spider swings from the rafters
to the oil painting; spider
crouches in my sneaker; spider
bobbles on the end of an escape
filament acrobatic over my type-
writer in front of my nose.

What do they eat? Not the mice
in the walls. Not the ants
busy on their rush-hour freeways
from the sugar cannister
and the olive oil spill to the secret
tunnel world under the sink.
Not the sowbugs, wee armadillos
nibbling the geranium leaves.
Not the wasps sleeping in paper
lanterns under the eaves. The other
nine hundred thousand inhabitants of what
I foolishly call my house.

The Listmaker

I am a compiler of lists: 1 bag
fine cracked corn, 1 sunflower seeds.

Thin tomato seedlings in hotbed;
check dahlias for sprouting.

Write Kathy. Call Lou. Pay
oil bill. Decide about Montana.

I find withered lists in pockets
of raincoats, reminders to buy birthday

presents for lovers who wear those warm
sweaters now in other lives. And what

did I decide about Montana? To believe
or disbelieve in its existence?

To rise at five some morning and fly there?
A buried assent or denial rots beneath.

I confess too that sometimes when I am listing
what I must do on a Monday, I will put on

tasks already completed for the neat pleasure
of striking them out, checking them off.

What do these lists mean? That I mistrust my memory,
that my attention, a huge hungry crow

settling to carrion even on the highway
hates to rise and flap off, wants to continue

feasting on what it has let down upon
folding the tent of its broad dusty wings.

That I like to conquer chaos one square
at a time like a board game.

That I fear the sins of omission more
than commission. That the whining saw

of the mill of time shrieks always in my ears
as I am borne with all the other logs

forward to be dismantled and rebuilt
into chairs, into frogs, into running water.

All lists start where they halt, in intention.
Only the love that is work completes them.

Going into town in the storm

The sky is white and the earth is white
and the white wind is blowing in arabesques

through us. The world wizens in the cold
to a circle that stops beyond my mittens

outstretched on which the white froth
still dissolves. Up, north, left—

all are obliterated in the swirl.
The only color that exists clings to

your face, your coat, your scarf.
We ride the feathered back of a white goose

that flies miles high over the Himalayas.
Where yesterday houses stood of neighbors,

summer people, scandals still smouldering—
heaps of old tires that burn for days—

today all is whited out, a mistake
on a typed page. My blood fizzes in my cheeks

like a shaken soda waiting to explode.
Into any haven we reach we will carry

a dizziness, a blindness that will melt
slowly, a sense of how uneasily we inhabit

this earth, how a rise or drop of a few degrees,
a little more water or a trifle less, renders

us strange as brontosaurus in our homeland.
We are fitted for a short winter and then spring.

We stagger out of the belly of the snow
plucked of words naked and steaming.

The clumsy season

I keep cutting off bits of my fingers or banging
my knee hard. I am offering pain and blood
like a down payment on myself withheld.

Don't leave me because I am wasting words,
pissing them out like bad wine swallowed
that leaves the skull echoing and scraped.

Don't let the words rise up and leave me
like a flight of dissatisfied geese.
I am waters waiting to be troubled again.

I am coming back and I will enter quiet
like a cave and crouch with my knees drawn up
till you birth me into squabbling bliss.

I promise to relearn stillness like a spider.
I will apprentice myself to pine trees.
I will study the heron waiting on one foot.

Only do not leave me empty as the skin
the snake has cast on the path, ghostly
colors fading and the sinuous hunter gone.

Fill me roaring with your necessary music.
Loose upon me your stories screaming for life,
ravenous as gulls over a fishing boat.

Or send the little dreams like gnats into my hair.
Tease me with almost vision, flashes, scents
that dangle barbs into the dark currents

of memory. Use me however you will but
use me. These little accidents are offerings
to that Coming never accidental.

Silk confetti

Apple blossom petals lay on asphalt
fallen from the tree at the road's turn
white as the flesh of the apple
will be, flushed pink
with the same blush
tender and curved as cheeks;
soft on hard; soon
to be bruised to vague stains.
Our best impulses often drop so
and vanish under traffic. We will
not know for months
if they bore fruit.

And whose creature am I?

At times characters from my novels swarm through me,
children of my mind, and possess me as dybbuks.
My own shabby memories they have plucked and eaten
till sometimes I cannot remember my own sorrows.
In all that I value there is a core of mystery,
in the seed that wriggles its new roots into the soil
and whose pale head bursts the surface,
in the dance where our bodies merge and reassemble,
in the starving baby whose huge glazing eyes
burned into my bones, in the look that passes
between predator and prey before the death blow.

I know of what rags and bones and clippings
from frothing newsprint and poisonous glue
my structures are built. Yet these creatures
I have improvised like golem walk off and thrive.
Between one and two thirds of our lives we spend
in darkness, and the little lights we turn on
make little holes in that great thick rich void.
We are never done with knowing or with gnawing,
but under the saying is whispering, touching
and silence. Out of a given set of atoms
we cast and recast the holy patterns new.

In praise of gazebos

Trellises bear the weight of roses,
pole beans, grape vines, wisteria,
yet a stake or posts with wires
strung between gives as good support.
They are expressions of pleasure,
garden jewelry, gestures
of proportion in the winter,
cascades of avid tangled greenery
in the full clamor of summer.

Benches under trees, cedar chairs
that overlook the tomatoes or the marsh
gradually ripening from green to sand
to bronze, a settee and table
on the grass, why do these furnishings
seem Victorian? We go out to play,
fiercely and with bats, with balls,
with rackets. We go out to bash our flesh
on the rough granite boulder of our will.

To sit among the shrubs and contemplate,
not for a tan, not for the body's
honing, oiling or toning, but just
to feed the eyes and scalded ears,
to let a gentle light into the brain,

to quiet the media babble, without radio,
Walkman, blast box, to let cool
the open hearth furnaces of ambition,
is to shape a space left open for calm

as if that harmony could shine down
like sunlight on the scalp. Perhaps
you say these little structures which contain
no real furniture, work or tools
are secret traps for catching silence.
Let outside and inside blur in the light season.
Build us pergolas, follies, arbors, terraces.
Let us make our gardens half artful
and half wild, to match our love.

The Faithless

Sleep, you jade smooth liar,
you promised to come
to me, come to me
waiting here like a cut
open melon ripe as summer.

Sleep, you black velvet
tomcat, where are you prowling?
I set a trap of sheets
clean and fresh as daisies,
pillows like cloudy sighs.

Sleep, you soft-bellied
angel with feathered thighs,
you tease my cheek with the brush
of your wings. I reach
for you but clutch air.

Sleep, you fur-bottomed tramp,
when I want you, you're in
everybody's bed but my own.
Take you for granted and you stalk
me from the low point of every hour.

Sleep, omnivorous billy goat,
you gobble the kittens, the crows,
the cop on duty, the fast horse,
but me you leave on the plate
like a cold shore dinner.

Is this divorce permanent?
Runneled with hope I lie down
nightly longing to pass
again under the fresh blessing
of your weight and broad wings.

If I had been called Sabrina or Ann, she said

I'm the only poet with the name.
Can you imagine a prima ballerina named
Marge? Marge Curie, Nobel Prize winner.
Empress Marge. My lady Marge? Rhymes with
large/charge/barge. Workingclass?
Definitely. Any attempt to doll it up
(Mar-gee? Mar-gette? Margelina?
Margarine?) makes it worse. Name
like an oilcan, like a bedroom
slipper, like a box of baking soda,
useful, plain; impossible for foreigners,
from French to Japanese, to pronounce.
My own grandmother called me what
could only be rendered in English
as Mousie. O my parents, what
you did unto me, forever. Even
my tombstone will look like a cartoon.

The night the moon got drunk

Up over the white shoulder of the dune
the sand that scorched our soles
now caresses our bare feet with cool compliance.
The foundry of the sun is shut down.
Where are the shallow caverns of shadow
carved into the blinding desert light?
Bowls of mist, pennons, traveling
ghosts. Finally the moon floats belly
up like a dead goldfish over the dune.
Tonight it could not get free
of the ocean wave but trails spume.
White as salt, it seems to be dissolving.
But it leers oddly. A tipsy moon
wobbling, wavering over the sand
as if it can't find the way up.

O drunken moon, you see too much
peering down: mugging, stabbing, rape,
the weak slipping into death,
the abandoned raking the ceiling
with the sharp claws of hunger.
You watch lovers in every hamlet,
in beds, in cars, in hammocks.
You cross the cranky Atlantic
and stuck up in the sky and lonely
what do you see first but couples
coupling on the Great Beach, among
the shiny poison ivy leaves
of the gentle slopes and sand tracks.
No wonder you drink yourself tipsy
on salt wine and go staggering now
faded and crooked, still lecherous.

Sweet ambush

We all await the blackberries,
stealthy as foxes, stopping by
in August disguised as
joggers, tourists, birdwatchers.

They begin hard and green,
baby hand-grenades. Slowly
they blush. The red
empurples like aging wine.

The day they first glint
with jet-bead shininess
somebody pounces. Losers
pick only the moldy and green.

Blackberrying: the tiger
hunting of scavenging.
Tonight even before I take
the pie from the oven,

its crisp lattice steaming,
my neighbor accuses, waving
her fork like a weapon,
You got blackberries today.

My arms are scored
as if by a lover too much
in a hurry to bother
with zippers and gentle tugs.

Smug after a successful
raid, I hold out arms
etched with hieroglyphs.
My mouth is purple inside.

Blueberries are gentle.
We squat among the bushes,
picking, picking, picking.
Only tedium limits our haul.

With each berry in its season
we wait to catch the very day
its flavor petal by petal
opens fully at last like a rose.

The high arch of summer

Light sharpens on the leaves
of cotoneaster, just as it sparks
off running water, shards of glitter
ticking the eyes glad. As I go down,
go down from the house, till it sinks
setting behind the hill, even in pine
woods the sun is hot to the bare sole
on the white sand path. Resin
thickens the air, invisible smoke.

Here I am at peace eating handfuls
of tart blueberries touched with bloom
as the morning was coated with fog
and huckleberries shiny and black
as the last moonless night. Here I laze
feeling the sun ripening my blood
sweet as the tomatoes near the house
in air that smells like air,
by water that tastes of water.

What we fail to notice

The crimson and fragrant musk roses,
the sweetest juicy blackberries,
rake the arms with their brambles,
slash the calves, but the small thorn
that slides into the skin covertly
unmarked by a bubble of blood
causes the real trouble
as the skin closes over
and its thin red line of infection
steals toward the heart.

Tashlich

Go to the ocean and throw the crumbs in,
all that remains of seven years.
When you wept, didn't I taste your tears
on my cheek, give you bread for salt?

Here where I sing at full pitch
and volume uncensored, I was attacked.
The pale sister nibbled like a mouse
in the closets with sharp pointy teeth.

She let herself in with her own key.
My trust garlanded her round. Indeed
it was convenient to trust her
while she wasted paper thin with envy.

Here she coveted. Here she crept.
Here her cold fluttering hands lingered
on secrets and dipped into the honey.
Her shadow fell on the contents of every drawer.

Alone in the house she made love
to herself in the mirror wearing
stolen gowns; then she carried them home
for their magic to color her life.

Little losses spread like tooth decay.
Furtive betrayals festered, cysts
hidden in flesh. Her greed swelled
in the dark, its hunger always roaring.

No number of gifts could silence
those cries of resentful hunger,
not for the baubles, the scarves,
the blouses she stole, but to be twenty

and pretty again, not to have to work
to live but merely to be blond and thin
and let men happen like rain in the night
and never to wake alone.

On the new year my grandmother Hannah
told me to carry crumbs to the water
and cast them out. We are tossing
away the trust that was too convenient

and we are throwing evil from the house
the rancid taint of envy spoiling the food
the pricing fingers of envy rumpling the cloth
the secret ill-wisher chewing from inside

the heart's red apple to rot it out.
I cast away my anger like spoiled milk.
Let the salty wind air the house and cleanse
the stain of betrayal from the new year.

This small and intimate place

1.

The moor land, the dry land ripples
bronzed with blueberry. The precise
small hills sculpted with glittering
kinnikinnick broil under the sharp
tack of the red-tailed hawk cruising
in middle air. A vesper sparrow
gives its repetitive shrill sad cry
and the air shimmers with drought.

The sea is always painting itself
on the sky, which dips low here.
Light floods the eyes tight and dry.
Light scours out the skull
like an old kitchen sink made clean.
We are cured in sunlight like salt cod.

2.

We are cured in sunlight like salt cod
stiffened and rot repellent and long
lived, long lasting. The year-rounders
are poor. All summer they wait tables
for the tourists, clean the houses
of the summer people, sell them jam, fish,
paintings, build their dwellings, wait
for the land to be clean and still again.

Yet blueberries, black- and elderberries,
beach plum grow where vacation homes

for psychiatrists are not yet built.
We gather oysters, dig clams. We burn
oak, locust, pitch pine and eat much fish
as do the other scavengers, the gulls.

3.

As do the other scavengers, the gulls,
we suffer, prey on the tides' rise and ebb
of plenty and disaster, the slick that chokes
the fisheries, the restaurant sewage
poisoning mussels, the dump leaching lead
into the water table; the lucky winter
storm that tosses up surf clams or squid
in heaps for food, fertilizer, future plenty.

This land is a tablet on which each pair
of heels writes itself, the raw scar
where the dirt bike crossed, the crushed
tern chicks where the ORV roared through,
the dune loosed over trodden grasses.
We are intimate with wind and water here.

4.

We are intimate with wind. Once
this was a land of windmills flapping

sails like a stationary race of yachts.
We learn the winds on face and shingles,
the warm wind off the Gulf Stream in winter,
the nor'easter piling up snow and wrecks,
the west wind that hustles the rain clouds
over and out to sea, the cold northwest.

We are intimate with water, lapped around,
the sea tearing at the land, castling it up,
damp salty days with grey underworld light
when sneakers mold like Roquefort, paper wilts.
On moors webbed in fog we wander, or wade
in the salt marsh as the wet lands ripple.

How grey, how wet, how cold

They are bits of fog caught in armor.
The outside pretends to the solidity of rocks
and requires force and skill bearing in
to cut the muscle, shatter the illusion.

If you stare at them, your stomach
curls, the grey eyes of Athene
pried out, the texture of heavy phlegm,
chill clots of mortality and come.

They lie on the tongue, distillations
of the sea. Fresh as the morning
wind that tatters the mist.
Sweet as cream but with that bottom

of granite, the taste of deep well
water drawn up on the hottest day,
the vein of slate in true Chablis,
the kiss of acid sharpening the tongue.

They slip down quick as minnows
darting to cover, and the mouth
remembers sex. Both provide
a meeting of the primitive

and worldly, in that we do
little more for oysters than the gull

smashing the shells on the rocks
or the crab wrestling them open,

yet in subtle flavor and the choice
to taste them raw comes a delicacy
not of the brain but of the senses
and the wit to leave perfection bare.

Deer couchant

Seen from the air, when the small plane
veers in and hangs for a moment
suspended like a gull in the wind,
the dune grass breathes,
hue of rabbit fur.
The waves are regular,
overlapping like fish scales.
The Cape in winter viewed
from above is a doe
of the small island race
lying down but not asleep,
the small delicate head
slightly lifted. She rests
from the ravages of the summer
as a deer will take her ease after
the season of rifles and boots.

Peaches in November

On the peach's wide sieve of branches
the buds crouch already in whitish caterpillar fur.

All winter they must hold tight, as the supple
limbs are strained wide by the snow's weight,

as the ice coats them and turns them to glinting
small lights that splinter the sun to prickles.

Must hold tight against the wet warm tongue
of the thaw that lolls off the Gulf Stream

smelling of seaweed and the South, as if
not spring visited but summer in January.

Hold tight against the early March sun
with the wild tulips already opening

against the brown earth like painted mouths
when the ice will return as a thief

to take what has too widely trusted.
The news they carry can only be told once

to the bees each year. The bud is the idea
of sweetness, of savor, of round heft

waiting to build itself. As the winter
clamps down they hibernate in fur,

little polar bears on red twigs
dreaming of turning one sun into many.

136

Six underrated pleasures

1. Folding sheets

They must be clean.
There ought to be two of you
to talk as you work, your
eyes and hands meeting.
They can be crisp, a little rough
and fragrant from the line;
or hot from the dryer
as from an oven. A silver
grey kitten with amber
eyes to dart among
the sheets and wrestle and leap out
helps. But mostly pleasure
lies in the clean linen
slapping into shape.
Whenever I fold a fitted sheet
making the moves that are like
closing doors, I feel my mother.
The smell of clean laundry is hers.

2. Picking pole beans

Gathering tomatoes has no art
to it. Their ripe redness shouts.
But the scarlet runner beans twine
high and jungly on their tripods.
You must reach in delicately,
pinch off the sizable beans
but leave the babies to swell

into flavor. It is hide-and-seek,
standing knee deep in squash
plants running, while the bees
must be carefully disentangled
from your hair. Early you may see
the hummingbird, but best to wait
until the dew burns off.
Basket on your arm, your fingers
go swimming through the raspy leaves
to find prey just their size.
Then comes the minor zest
of nipping the ends off with your nails
and snapping them in pieces,
their retorts like soft pistolry.
Then eat the littlest raw.

3. Taking a hot bath

Surely nobody has ever decided
to go on a diet while in a tub.
The body is beautiful stretched
out under water wavering.

It suggests a long island of pleasure
whole seascapes of calm sensual
response, the nerves as gentle fronds
of waterweed swaying in warm currents.

Then if ever we must love ourselves
in the amniotic fluid floating

a ship at anchor in a perfect
protected blood-warm tropical bay.

The water enters us and the minor
pains depart, supplanted guests,
the aches, the strains, the chills.
Muscles open like hungry clams.

Born again from my bath like a hot
sweet-tempered, sweet-smelling baby,
I am ready to seize sleep like a milky breast
or start climbing my day hand over hand.

4. Sleeping with cats

I am at once source
and sink of heat: giver
and taker. I am a vast
soft mountain of slow breathing.
The smells I exude soothe them:
the lingering odor of sex,
of soap, even of perfume,
its afteraroma sunk into skin
mingling with sweat and the traces
of food and drink.

They are curled into flowers
of fur, they are coiled
hot seashells of flesh
in my armpit, around my head

a dark sighing halo.
They are plastered to my side,
a poultice fixing sore muscles
better than a heating pad.
They snuggle up to my sex
purring. They embrace my feet.

Some cats I place like a pillow.
In the morning they rest where
I arranged them, still sleeping.
Some cats start at my head
and end between my legs
like a textbook lover. Some
slip out to prowl the living room
patrolling, restive, then
leap back to fight about
hegemony over my knees.

Every one of them cares
passionately where they sleep
and with whom.
Sleeping together is a euphemism
for people but tantamount
to marriage for cats.
Mammals together we snuggle
and snore through the cold nights
while the stars swing round
the pole and the great horned
owl hunts for flesh like ours.

5. Planting bulbs

No task could be easier.
Just dig the narrow hole,
drop in the handful of bone
meal and place the bulb
like a swollen brown garlic
clove full of hidden resources.

Their skin is the paper
of brown bags. The smooth
pale flesh peeks through.
Three times its height
is its depth, a parable
against hard straining.

The art is imagining
the spring landscape poking
through chrysanthemum, falling
leaves, withered brown lushness
of summer. The lines drawn
now, the colors mixed

will pop out of the soil
after the snow sinks from sight
into it. The circles,
the casual grace of tossed handfuls,
the soldierly rows will stand,
the colors sing sweet or sour.

When the first sharp ears
poke out, you are again
more audience than actor,

as if someone said, Close
your eyes and draw a picture.
Now open them and look.

6. Canning

We pour a mild drink each,
turn on the record player,
Beethoven perhaps or Vivaldi,
opera sometimes, and then together
in the steamy kitchen we put up
tomatoes, peaches, grapes, pears.

Each fruit has a different
ritual: popping the grapes
out of the skins like little
eyeballs, slipping the fuzz
from the peaches and seeing
the blush painted on the flesh beneath.

It is part game: What shall
we magic wand this into?
Peach conserve, chutney, jam,
brandied peaches. Tomatoes
turn juice, sauce hot or mild
or spicy, canned, ketchup.

Vinegars, brandies, treats
for the winter: pleasure
deferred. Canning is thrift
itself in sensual form,

surplus made beautiful, light
and heat caught in a jar.

I find my mother sometimes
issuing from the steam, aproned,
red faced, her hair up in a net.
Since her death we meet usually
in garden or kitchen. Ghosts
come reliably to savors, I learn.

In the garden your ashes,
in the kitchen your knowledge.
Little enough we can save
from the furnace of the sun
while the bones grow brittle as paper
and the hair itself turns ashen.

But what we can put by, we do
with gaiety and invention
while the music laps round us
like dancing light, but Mother,
this pleasure is only deferred.
We eat it all before it spoils.

A note about the author

Marge Piercy is the author of nine books of poetry: *Breaking Camp,
Hard Loving, 4-Telling, To Be of Use, Living in the Open, The
Twelve-Spoked Wheel Flashing, The Moon Is Always Female, Circles
on the Water*, and *Stone, Paper, Knife*. She has also published eight
novels: *Going Down Fast, Dance the Eagle to Sleep, Small Changes,
Woman on the Edge of Time, The High Cost of Living, Vida, Braided
Lives*, and *Away Home*. The University of Michigan's Arbor Press
published a volume of her essays, reviews, and interviews as part of
the Poets on Poetry Series entitled *Parti-Colored Blocks for a Quilt*.
She has also coauthored a play, *The Last White Class*, with her
husband, Ira Wood. She and Ira Wood live in Wellfleet,
Massachusetts.

A note on the type

This book was set on the Linotype in Century Expanded, designed in 1894 by Linn Boyd Benton (1844–1932). Benton cut Century Expanded in response to Theodore De Vinne's request for an attractive, easy-to-read typeface to fit the narrow columns of his *Century Magazine*. Early in the nineteen hundreds Morris Fuller Benton updated and improved Century in several versions for his father's American Type Founders Company. Century remains the only American typeface cut before 1910 still widely in use today.

Composed, printed, and bound by The Maple-Vail Book Manufacturing Group, Inc., Binghamton, New York, and York, Pennsylvania. Typography and binding design by Virginia Tan.